Our Sharing Journal: Journaling Notebook for Parents and Kids

M. Susan T. Whitehead

DEDICATION

This book is dedicated to my children, Joy, Marin, Brynne, Caralyn, Grant and Asher, who are an endless source of questions and inspiration…but mostly LOTS of questions!

M. Susan T. Whitehead

CONTENTS

ACKNOWLEDGMENTS

I would be a foolish woman to think I could do any of this without the unending support of my husband, Michael. I truly can't think of anything I've thrown at him that he hasn't supported me in and he has NEVER uttered the words, "I told you so." His patience and love is one that surpasses my understanding and sustains me when I fall flat on my face in failures.

Secondly, I must thank my mom and her example of unconditional love. No matter what my decisions have been, and even if she doesn't agree with them, she has demonstrated that there is nothing I can do to make her love me less. I pray this is something I pass on to my children and their future families.

My dad, who passed away in 2013 from cancer due to exposure to Agent Orange in the Vietnam War, was my constant cheerleader when it came to entrepreneurial adventures. I could always count on him to be super excited about any new venture or project I embarked upon. Making him proud has, and will continue to be, a driving force behind every new project or business idea I undertake.

Joy, Marin, Brynne, Caralyn, Grant and Asher, I am thankful for you letting me be your Mommy, while also picking up the slack when I needed help. You all are my greatest accomplishments and my life would truly be empty without each one of you.

M. Susan T. Whitehead

Why & How to Use This Journal

Before I explain anything about how to use this journal, I need you to promise ONE thing for me: NEVER USE THIS JOURNAL AS PUNISHMENT OR HOMEWORK! If you bought this in hopes of tricking your kids into doing supplementary writing, I'd like to ask you to close the book now and give it to a friend, neighbor, family member...anyone that has a child. That is not the purpose behind this book.

Now that's out of the way, I am so thankful to you for purchasing this book. When my oldest daughters were very young, maybe 5 and 3 years old, they liked to ask me the following question: "Mommy, can you tell me a story when you were a little girl?"

Sweet, isn't it? Well, when this question gets thrown at you multiple times a day, every day, the "sweetness" quickly fades and becomes a bit of an annoyance. As a young mother with little ones, I didn't realize at the time that what they really wanted was to connect with me in ways that made sense to them.

Those little brown eyed faces weren't trying to push my buttons (well, not all the time). Asking questions is the way they learn about the world and being their Mommy, I am part of the world they were and are still learning about. Being the person that spent the most time with them, I just happened to be the one who got the majority of the questions.

As our family grew, the questions never stopped coming. My husband also got his fair share of questions. I remember once hearing our girls ask their Daddy to tell them a story when he was a little GIRL. Of course, laughter ensued, but Daddy didn't escape the questioning.

My husband and I often joke that we can't get 30 seconds in our home without someone asking us something. With 6 children from almost 18 to 2, questions span the spectrum from "What are we having for dinner?" to deeper questions about death, life and the afterlife. Because we've always been open to questions from our children, we have cultivated an environment where our children feel safe asking us anything and everything.

My hope is that using this book will open the door to more communication between parents and their children. Our lives are so busy, whether due to work or school schedules, sporting events, music lessons and other activities, that just having a simple conversation with our children can be squashed.

Of course, none of us ever intend to push these moments aside, but they seem to be happening more and more, especially since we have become increasingly attached to our electronic devices. I'm the first to admit that I need to put my phone down and tuck my laptop away more. The solution I have come up with to force myself to do an "electronic fast" is by scheduling time to be fully present with my kids…without any distractions.

I'm not naïve enough to think a little book can dramatically change the dynamics of communication with your children, but my hope is that it will be fun enough for you AND your kids that you'll carve out some time to make getting to know each other more of a part of your daily lives.

So how should you use the journal? Remember the opening statement on the first page? The one about not using this book as punishment or homework? Yes, that's how I do not want you using this book. Trying to engage your children in thoughtful or even silly conversation should never be equated with punishment or work. Try to make it enjoyable and the results will be very worthwhile.

If you have trouble getting your child on board with going through the journal on his/her own, try incorporating it into your daily morning or evening routine. Instead of pushing them to write an answer, maybe you can just read the question and listen to the answer, jotting it down for him or her. Have crayons or color pencils handy and let them use the Doodle Space on each page to draw something.

Our second daughter and oldest son are kinesthetic learners, meaning they learn/retain information best when they're doing some sort of movement. I remember my husband getting frustrated during our family story time when our second daughter would not sit still on the couch to listen to him read a book. It wasn't until I gave her a doll to play with quietly on the floor or gave her some crayons and a coloring book that she could participate without being a major distraction. After the first time trying this new tactic during story time, we asked her about the story and she answered every question perfectly. Prior to that, she could barely remember the main topic or character.

Knowing your child's individual learning styles can really help you make the most of the journal. The book that helped me the most was The Way They Learn by Cynthia Ulrich Tobias. (Ironically, I am not a big reader, but this book really captivated me because I saw so many "misbehaviors" in a new light.) There are many other resources available online for finding out what style of learning your child uses, so I encourage you to do some research. Usually, the style is pretty obvious, but if your child spends most of his or her time in school or with someone else, it might help to give them a short quiz.

Often times, behavioral issues in a formal school setting stem not from a child who wants to misbehave, but one whose learning style just doesn't pair well with sitting still at a desk most of the day. While we have chosen to homeschool our children, that doesn't necessarily solve the problem of misbehaving. I wish I could say I had the answer to that, but I don't...and that would be an entirely different book! My main reason for bringing this up is that you might have one idea in your head about how to use the journal, but your child might need you to use it in a different way. Neither way needs to be "right or wrong" because we're all uniquely wired. Playing to each of our strengths will nurture your relationship more than if one is forced to do things "my way".

Every family will have their own way of integrating this journal into their days, but finding a way that both of you will use it is the best place to start. If you have some down time in the morning before breakfast or before heading out the door to school, set aside 5 minutes to answer ONE question.

If you have more than 5 minutes, try to dig a little deeper into that ONE question. Some of us who value time and productivity will want to squeeze in as many questions as possible, but I know for a fact that too much of a good thing can quickly turn into a bad thing. In our house, that usually ends up with a frustrated mom and a grumpy child who just wants to run away and play.

Do you remember Pepé le Pew from Looney Tunes? He was the skunk that fell in love with the black and white cat and did everything he could to keep her close to him. His intentions were good, he was in love after all, but his desires to keep her close made him oblivious to her desires to get away. He ended up not receiving love in return from the cat because he didn't pay attention to what the cat was communicating.

The same thing can be said about how we communicate with our children. I'm sometimes known to go on and on when I'm talking about a subject I'm interested in OR when talking about a topic I think my children need to learn about more. The sad things is that I usually see the blank stare and closed off body language long before I stop talking. I don't know why I keep going because I know full well I've lost them. I am getting better. I just need to keep reminding myself that less talking on my part is often more when it comes to having a good conversation with my children.

If working the journal into your mornings doesn't work (I'm not fully awake until at least 9:30am!), you could try asking questions during a family meal. Use the last few minutes after finishing a meal and before cleaning up to bring out the book and answer the questions. You could also use it during your bed time routine. Basically, any time you'll do it is a good time.

What if you and your child are on a completely different schedule? Maybe you work nights or even live in separate homes? For shy children, sitting down and going through the questions together might not be ideal. You can each work on your questions separately and then leave the book in a central spot where the other person can come along and pick it up when they can.

In this case, when you don't go through each question together, you can gently ask your child if they've had a chance to answer the next question. Don't make it a requirement or make it seem like just one more thing they have to do. It might mean you taking it out and reading what you wrote in an effort to peak their interest and answer the question, too.

As you go through the book, remember there are no wrong answers. Try not to focus on mistakes like grammar or spelling, as that can quickly take the fun out of it. If you model proper grammar and spelling in your own answers, it's not unlikely that your child will notice the differences and make corrections. Constantly pointing out our child's errors is a fast track to failure in communication. Remember that this is not school work.

The journal also does not have to be used from cover to cover. There is no set order of the questions except that I tried to space similar ones more than 1 day apart. The only thing I do encourage is that you and your child answer the same question at the same time. This way, it can promote discussions of why each of you chose your responses.

Each page also has a Doodle Space on it. You can use this space however you like. Write a note to your child about something good you caught them doing. Let them know how amazing they are or how much you enjoy using the journal together. Draw a funny picture. It's your space to play!

At the very end of the book, I ask both of you to write about something that really stood out to you through the whole process. Maybe you learned that your child likes raisins in his salad or would rather live in the "wilderness, like on Survivor", as my 7 year old told me. (Sorry Buddy, not going to happen with me!) After going through an experience like this, I thought it would be a fun thing to look back and reflect on the things you found out about each other.

So that's basically it! Grab a pen or pencil or crayons and get going. Remember, just one question a day. No spell check. No criticism and no wrong answers. Have fun with a new way of communicating with your child. They don't stay young forever.

M. Susan T. Whitehead

Let the Journaling Begin!

What are the 3 best things about you?

_____

_____

_____

_____

_____

_____

_____

_____

Doodle Space

What are the 3 best things about you?

_____

_____

_____

_____

_____

_____

_____

_____

_____

Doodle Space

If you could ask to never eat 2 foods ever again, which ones would you pick?

_____

_____

_____

_____

_____

_____

_____

_____

Doodle Space

If you could ask to never eat 2 foods ever again, which ones would you pick?

_____

_____

_____

_____

_____

_____

_____

Doodle Space

Would you rather live in a tropical rain forest or a desert? Why?

_____

_____

_____

_____

_____

_____

_____

_____

Doodle Space

Would you rather live in a tropical rain forest or a desert? Why?

_____

_____

_____

_____

_____

_____

_____

_____

_____

Doodle Space

What can make you smile, no matter what?

_____

_____

_____

_____

_____

_____

_____

_____

Doodle Space

What can make you smile, no matter what?

_____

_____

_____

_____

_____

_____

_____

_____

_____

Doodle Space

What is your favorite article of clothing?

_____

_____

_____

_____

_____

_____

_____

_____

_____

Doodle Space

What is your favorite article of clothing?

_____

_____

_____

_____

_____

_____

_____

_____

Doodle Space

If you could only wear 2 colors the rest of your life, which colors would they be?

_____

_____

_____

_____

_____

_____

_____

_____

Doodle Space

If you could only wear 2 colors the rest of your life, which colors would they be?

_____

_____

_____

_____

_____

_____

_____

_____

Doodle Space

What is your favorite restaurant and what is your favorite thing to eat there?

_____

_____

_____

_____

_____

_____

_____

_____

_____

Doodle Space

What is your favorite restaurant and what is your favorite thing to eat there?

_____

_____

_____

_____

_____

_____

_____

_____

_____

Doodle Space

If you could go anywhere in the universe, but had to leave right now, where would you go?

_____

_____

_____

_____

_____

_____

_____

_____

_____

Doodle Space

If you could go anywhere in the universe, but had to leave right now, where would you go?

_____

_____

_____

_____

_____

_____

_____

_____

_____

Doodle Space

If you were granted ONE wish, which one would you chose: a genius, a famous athlete, or a rich business owner?

_____

_____

_____

_____

_____

_____

_____

Doodle Space

If you were granted ONE wish, which one would you chose: a genius, a famous athlete, or a rich business owner?

_____

_____

_____

_____

_____

_____

_____

Doodle Space

When you're feeling sad, what can I do to help you feel better?

_____

_____

_____

_____

_____

_____

_____

_____

_____

Doodle Space

When you're feeling sad, what can I do to help you feel better?

_____

_____

_____

_____

_____

_____

_____

_____

_____

Doodle Space

Trace your toes on the Doodle Space and write a word on each toe that describes how you've felt today.

Doodle Space

Trace your toes on the Doodle Space and write a word on each toe that describes how you've felt today.

Doodle Space

What is your favorite song to sing REALLY loudly?

_____

_____

_____

_____

_____

_____

_____

_____

Doodle Space

What is your favorite song to sing REALLY loudly?

_____

_____

_____

_____

_____

_____

_____

_____

Doodle Space

What makes you a good friend and why?

_____

_____

_____

_____

_____

_____

_____

_____

Doodle Space

What makes you a good friend and why?

_____

_____

_____

_____

_____

_____

_____

_____

Doodle Space

Which chore is your least favorite and why?

_____

_____

_____

_____

_____

_____

_____

_____

Doodle Space

Which chore is your least favorite and why?

_____

_____

_____

_____

_____

_____

_____

_____

Doodle Space

What is your favorite toy or thing that you own?

_____

_____

_____

_____

_____

_____

_____

_____

_____

Doodle Space

What is your favorite toy or thing that you own?

_____

_____

_____

_____

_____

_____

_____

_____

_____

Doodle Space

What is the most beautiful thing you've ever seen?

_____

_____

_____

_____

_____

_____

_____

_____

_____

Doodle Space

Our Sharing Journal

What is the most beautiful thing you've ever seen?

_____

_____

_____

_____

_____

_____

_____

_____

_____

Doodle Space

45

What would you do if you saw someone steal something at a store?

_____

_____

_____

_____

_____

_____

_____

_____

_____

Doodle Space

What would you do if you saw someone steal something at a store?

_____

_____

_____

_____

_____

_____

_____

_____

_____

Doodle Space

If you had to pick one of these jobs, which would you like to do most: fire fighter, doctor, teacher or police officer? Why?

_____

_____

_____

_____

_____

_____

_____

_____

Doodle Space

If you had to pick one of these jobs, which would you like to do most: fire fighter, doctor, teacher or police officer? Why?

_____

_____

_____

_____

_____

_____

_____

Doodle Space

If you were a spy, what would be your spy name and why?

_____

_____

_____

_____

_____

_____

_____

_____

Doodle Space

If you were a spy, what would be your spy name and why?

_____

_____

_____

_____

_____

_____

_____

_____

Doodle Space

What makes someone a good parent?

_____

_____

_____

_____

_____

_____

_____

_____

_____

Doodle Space

What makes someone a good parent?

_____

_____

_____

_____

_____

_____

_____

_____

_____

Doodle Space

If we didn't have any money for presents for your birthday, what would you like to do?

_____

_____

_____

_____

_____

_____

_____

_____

_____

Doodle Space

If we didn't have any money for presents for your birthday, what would you like to do?

_____

_____

_____

_____

_____

_____

_____

_____

_____

Doodle Space

What is your favorite movie and why?

_____

_____

_____

_____

_____

_____

_____

_____

_____

_____

Doodle Space

What is your favorite movie and why?

_____

_____

_____

_____

_____

_____

_____

_____

_____

_____

Doodle Space

If we could do something together, just the two of us, what would you like to do?

_____

_____

_____

_____

_____

_____

_____

_____

_____

Doodle Space

If we could do something together, just the two of us, what would you like to do?

_____

_____

_____

_____

_____

_____

_____

_____

_____

Doodle Space

What is your favorite way to make art: paint, markers, crayons, color pencils?

_____

_____

_____

_____

_____

_____

_____

_____

_____

Doodle Space

What is your favorite way to make art: paint, markers, crayons, color pencils?

_____

_____

_____

_____

_____

_____

_____

_____

_____

Doodle Space

Name 2 things you would like to change about your room and why.

_____

_____

_____

_____

_____

_____

_____

_____

Doodle Space

Name 2 things you would like to change about your room and why.

_____

_____

_____

_____

_____

_____

_____

_____

Doodle Space

If you could go into space, would you? Where would you like to go?

_____

_____

_____

_____

_____

_____

_____

_____

_____

Doodle Space

If you could go into space, would you? Where would you like to go?

_____

_____

_____

_____

_____

_____

_____

_____

_____

Doodle Space

If you could talk to one animal and understand them, which animal would you pick and what would you ask?

_____

_____

_____

_____

_____

_____

_____

_____

Doodle Space

If you could talk to one animal and understand them, which animal would you pick and what would you ask?

_____

_____

_____

_____

_____

_____

_____

Doodle Space

If you could live somewhere else, where would you choose and why?

_____

_____

_____

_____

_____

_____

_____

_____

_____

Doodle Space

If you could live somewhere else, where would you choose and why?

_____

_____

_____

_____

_____

_____

_____

_____

_____

Doodle Space

Have you ever had a really scary dream? What was it about?

Doodle Space

Have you ever had a really scary dream? What was it about?

_____

_____

_____

_____

_____

_____

_____

_____

_____

Doodle Space

What is the weirdest pet you would want to have and what would you call it?

_____

_____

_____

_____

_____

_____

_____

_____

Doodle Space

What is the weirdest pet you would want to have and what would you call it?

_____

_____

_____

_____

_____

_____

_____

_____

Doodle Space

If you could live somewhere else, where would you choose and why?

_____

_____

_____

_____

_____

_____

_____

_____

_____

Doodle Space

If you could live somewhere else, where would you choose and why?

_____

_____

_____

_____

_____

_____

_____

_____

_____

Doodle Space

If you met someone new that has never met me before, how would you describe me?

_____

_____

_____

_____

_____

_____

_____

_____

Doodle Space

If you met someone new that has never met me before, how would you describe me?

_____

_____

_____

_____

_____

_____

_____

_____

Doodle Space

Do you like to be inside or outside more? Why?

_____

_____

_____

_____

_____

_____

_____

_____

Doodle Space

Do you like to be inside or outside more? Why?

_____

_____

_____

_____

_____

_____

_____

_____

_____

Doodle Space

What is the grossest thing you've ever eaten? Why was it so gross?

_____

_____

_____

_____

_____

_____

_____

_____

_____

Doodle Space

What is the grossest thing you've ever eaten? Why was it so gross?

_____

_____

_____

_____

_____

_____

_____

_____

_____

Doodle Space

If you could trade lives with anyone, who would you choose and why?

_____

_____

_____

_____

_____

_____

_____

_____

_____

Doodle Space

If you could trade lives with anyone, who would you choose and why?

_____

_____

_____

_____

_____

_____

_____

_____

_____

Doodle Space

Do you think any of our neighbors are scary or mean? Who and why?

_____

_____

_____

_____

_____

_____

_____

_____

_____

Doodle Space

Do you think any of our neighbors are scary or mean? Who and why?

_____

_____

_____

_____

_____

_____

_____

_____

_____

Doodle Space

Which family member do you get along with the best?

_____

_____

_____

_____

_____

_____

_____

_____

_____

Doodle Space

Which family member do you get along with the best?

_____

_____

_____

_____

_____

_____

_____

_____

_____

Doodle Space

If you could be President, why would people like you?

_____

_____

_____

_____

_____

_____

_____

_____

_____

Doodle Space

If you could be President, why would people like you?

_____

_____

_____

_____

_____

_____

_____

_____

Doodle Space

What is one problem you've seen in our town that you would like to fix and why?

_____

_____

_____

_____

_____

_____

_____

_____

Doodle Space

What is one problem you've seen in our town that you would like to fix and why?

_____

_____

_____

_____

_____

_____

_____

_____

Doodle Space

Who in our family do you think you are the most like and in what ways?

_____

_____

_____

_____

_____

_____

_____

_____

_____

Doodle Space

Who in our family do you think you are the most like and in what ways?

_____

_____

_____

_____

_____

_____

_____

_____

_____

Doodle Space

Pretend you meet an alien from another galaxy. What would you tell them is the best part about living on Earth?

_____

_____

_____

_____

_____

_____

_____

Doodle Space

Pretend you meet an alien from another galaxy. What would you tell them is the best part about living on Earth?

_____

_____

_____

_____

_____

_____

_____

_____

Doodle Space

If you lost one of your senses, which one would be the most difficult to live without? Sight, Hearing, Taste, Touch or Smell

_____

_____

_____

_____

_____

_____

_____

Doodle Space

If you lost one of your senses, which one would be the most difficult to live without? Sight, Hearing, Taste, Touch or Smell

_____

_____

_____

_____

_____

_____

_____

Doodle Space

Why do you think some people don't like to have pets?

_____

_____

_____

_____

_____

_____

_____

_____

Doodle Space

Why do you think some people don't like to have pets?

_____

_____

_____

_____

_____

_____

_____

_____

_____

Doodle Space

Name one thing you remember from when you were really young.

_____

_____

_____

_____

_____

_____

_____

_____

_____

Doodle Space

Name one thing you remember from when you were really young.

_____

_____

_____

_____

_____

_____

_____

_____

_____

Doodle Space

Is there anything you're really afraid of? Why?

_____

_____

_____

_____

_____

_____

_____

_____

_____

Doodle Space

Is there anything you're really afraid of? Why?

_____

_____

_____

_____

_____

_____

_____

_____

_____

Doodle Space

M. Susan T. Whitehead

If you became invisible for one day, what would you do?

Doodle Space

If you became invisible for one day, what would you do?

_____

_____

_____

_____

_____

_____

_____

_____

_____

Doodle Space

What would you do if we went shopping and got separated and couldn't find each other?

_____

_____

_____

_____

_____

_____

_____

_____

_____

Doodle Space

What would you do if we went shopping and got separated and couldn't find each other?

_____

_____

_____

_____

_____

_____

_____

_____

_____

Doodle Space

Do you think you're as intelligent as your friends? Why or why not?

_____

_____

_____

_____

_____

_____

_____

_____

_____

_____

Doodle Space

Do you think you're as intelligent as your friends? Why or why not?

_____

_____

_____

_____

_____

_____

_____

_____

_____

Doodle Space

What talent do you have that you're proud of?

_____

_____

_____

_____

_____

_____

_____

_____

_____

Doodle Space

What talent do you have that you're proud of?

_____

_____

_____

_____

_____

_____

_____

_____

Doodle Space

If you could be a super hero, what would your super power be?

_____

_____

_____

_____

_____

_____

_____

_____

_____

Doodle Space

If you could be a super hero, what would your super power be?

_____

_____

_____

_____

_____

_____

_____

_____

Doodle Space

What are your favorite things to do on a rainy day?

_____

_____

_____

_____

_____

_____

_____

_____

Doodle Space

What are your favorite things to do on a rainy day?

_____

_____

_____

_____

_____

_____

_____

_____

Doodle Space

Which country sounds the most interesting to visit?

_____

_____

_____

_____

_____

_____

_____

_____

_____

Doodle Space

Which country sounds the most interesting to visit?

_____

_____

_____

_____

_____

_____

_____

_____

Doodle Space

If you could be really good at a musical instrument, which one would you choose?

_____

_____

_____

_____

_____

_____

_____

_____

Doodle Space

If you could be really good at a musical instrument, which one would you choose?

_____

_____

_____

_____

_____

_____

_____

_____

_____

Doodle Space

What are your favorite toppings for pizza? Which toppings do you dislike most?

_____

_____

_____

_____

_____

_____

_____

_____

_____

Doodle Space

What are your favorite toppings for pizza? Which toppings do you dislike most?

_____

_____

_____

_____

_____

_____

_____

Doodle Space

M. Susan T. Whitehead

If you had to choose between spending a week in the mountains or a week at the beach, which would you pick? What would you do there?

_____

_____

_____

_____

_____

_____

_____

_____

Doodle Space

If you had to choose between spending a week in the mountains or a week at the beach, which would you pick? What would you do there?

_____

_____

_____

_____

_____

_____

_____

_____

_____

Doodle Space

Describe your perfect salad including vegetables, fruits, meats, cheeses, salad dressings and other toppings.

_____

_____

_____

_____

_____

_____

_____

_____

_____

_____

Doodle Space

Describe your perfect salad including vegetables, fruits, meats, cheeses, salad dressings and other toppings.

_____

_____

_____

_____

_____

_____

_____

_____

_____

_____

Doodle Space

Do you think your name fits you? If so, why? If not, which name do you think fits you best?

_____

_____

_____

_____

_____

_____

_____

_____

_____

Doodle Space

Do you think your name fits you? If so, why? If not, which name do you think fits you best?

_____

_____

_____

_____

_____

_____

_____

_____

_____

Doodle Space

Do you think working in an office would be something you'd like to do? Why or why not?

_____

_____

_____

_____

_____

_____

_____

_____

_____

Doodle Space

Do you think working in an office would be something you'd like to do? Why or why not?

_____

_____

_____

_____

_____

_____

_____

_____

_____

Doodle Space

If you could choose where we lived, would you like to be in a big city apartment, a farm out in the country, or in a neighborhood with a nearby playground? Or somewhere completely different? Use the Doodle Space to draw your pick.

Doodle Space

If you could choose where we lived, would you like to be in a big city apartment, a farm out in the country, or in a neighborhood with a nearby playground?   Or somewhere completely different? Use the Doodle Space to draw your pick.

Doodle Space

What is your favorite subject in school? Do you think you're good at it?

_____

_____

_____

_____

_____

_____

_____

_____

_____

Doodle Space

What is your favorite subject in school? Do you think you're good at it?

_____

_____

_____

_____

_____

_____

_____

_____

_____

Doodle Space

Do you think working in an office would be something you'd like to do? Why or why not?

_____

_____

_____

_____

_____

_____

_____

_____

_____

Doodle Space

Do you think working in an office would be something you'd like to do? Why or why not?

_____

_____

_____

_____

_____

_____

_____

_____

_____

Doodle Space

Have you ever dreamt about being able to fly? What do you think would be the most fun?

_____

_____

_____

_____

_____

_____

_____

_____

_____

Doodle Space

Have you ever dreamt about being able to fly? What do you think would be the most fun?

_____

_____

_____

_____

_____

_____

_____

_____

_____

Doodle Space

Do you think you're an early bird or night owl? Would you like to be the other one? Why or why not?

_____

_____

_____

_____

_____

_____

_____

_____

_____

Doodle Space

Do you think you're an early bird or night owl? Would you like to be the other one? Why or why not?

_____

_____

_____

_____

_____

_____

_____

_____

_____

Doodle Space

What is your favorite holiday and why?

_____

_____

_____

_____

_____

_____

_____

_____

_____

Doodle Space

What is your favorite holiday and why?

_____

_____

_____

_____

_____

_____

_____

_____

_____

Doodle Space

Do you like to dance? What is your best dance move?

_____

_____

_____

_____

_____

_____

_____

_____

_____

Doodle Space

Do you like to dance? What is your best dance move?

_____

_____

_____

_____

_____

_____

_____

_____

_____

Doodle Space

Which season is your favorite and why? Spring, Summer, Fall or Winter? You can draw a picture, too.

_____

_____

_____

_____

_____

_____

_____

_____

_____

Doodle Space

Which season is your favorite and why? Spring, Summer, Fall or Winter? You can draw a picture, too.

_____

_____

_____

_____

_____

_____

_____

_____

_____

Doodle Space

What is your favorite thing to do at a park or playground?

_____

_____

_____

_____

_____

_____

_____

_____

Doodle Space

What is your favorite thing to do at a park or playground?

_____

_____

_____

_____

_____

_____

_____

_____

_____

Doodle Space

What is the best gift you've ever given?

_____

_____

_____

_____

_____

_____

_____

_____

Doodle Space

What is the best gift you've ever given?

_____

_____

_____

_____

_____

_____

_____

_____

_____

Doodle Space

If you had to plan our meals for an entire day, what would you plan? Try to include healthy things like fruits and veggies.

_____

_____

_____

_____

_____

_____

_____

_____

_____

_____

Doodle Space

If you had to plan our meals for an entire day, what would you plan? Try to include healthy things like fruits and veggies.

_____

_____

_____

_____

_____

_____

_____

_____

_____

Doodle Space

Describe your favorite ice cream. What flavor is it? Do you like it in a cup, cone or something else? Do you add any toppings like nuts, sprinkles or whipped cream?

_____

_____

_____

_____

_____

_____

_____

_____

_____

Doodle Space

Describe your favorite ice cream. What flavor is it? Do you like it in a cup, cone or something else? Do you add any toppings like nuts, sprinkles or whipped cream?

_____

_____

_____

_____

_____

_____

_____

_____

_____

Doodle Space

What is the best gift you've ever gotten?

_____

_____

_____

_____

_____

_____

_____

_____

Doodle Space

What is the best gift you've ever gotten?

_____

_____

_____

_____

_____

_____

_____

_____

_____

Doodle Space

Do you feel happy most days? Why or why not?

_____

_____

_____

_____

_____

_____

_____

_____

_____

Doodle Space

Do you feel happy most days? Why or why not?

_____

_____

_____

_____

_____

_____

_____

_____

_____

Doodle Space

What is something you could do to help keep our home cleaner?

_____

_____

_____

_____

_____

_____

_____

_____

Doodle Space

What is something you could do to help keep our home cleaner?

_____

_____

_____

_____

_____

_____

_____

_____

_____

Doodle Space

Which animal do you like the most at a zoo? Which do you like least? Why?

_____

_____

_____

_____

_____

_____

_____

_____

_____

Doodle Space

Which animal do you like the most at a zoo? Which do you like least? Why?

_____

_____

_____

_____

_____

_____

_____

_____

Doodle Space

How does it make you feel when you see a homeless person?

_____

_____

_____

_____

_____

_____

_____

_____

_____

_____

Doodle Space

How does it make you feel when you see a homeless person?

_____

_____

_____

_____

_____

_____

_____

_____

_____

_____

Doodle Space

Would you rather be a deep sea explorer or an astronaut? What would you like most about the one you chose?

_____

_____

_____

_____

_____

_____

_____

_____

_____

Doodle Space

Would you rather be a deep sea explorer or an astronaut? What would you like most about the one you chose?

_____

_____

_____

_____

_____

_____

_____

_____

_____

Doodle Space

If you could help an elderly person we know with some chores around their house, which one would you like to help with? Yard work? Cleaning the bathroom? Vacuuming? Some-thing else?

_____

_____

_____

_____

_____

_____

_____

_____

Doodle Space

If you could help an elderly person we know with some chores around their house, which one would you like to help with? Yard work? Cleaning the bathroom? Vacuuming? Some-thing else?

_____

_____

_____

_____

_____

_____

_____

Doodle Space

What is your favorite outfit to wear when you're not feeling well? What else do you like to have around you when you're sick?

_____

_____

_____

_____

_____

_____

_____

_____

_____

Doodle Space

What is your favorite outfit to wear when you're not feeling well? What else do you like to have around you when you're sick?

_____

_____

_____

_____

_____

_____

_____

_____

_____

Doodle Space

Who is the smartest person you know? What makes them so smart?

_____

_____

_____

_____

_____

_____

_____

_____

Doodle Space

Who is the smartest person you know? What makes them so smart?

_____

_____

_____

_____

_____

_____

_____

_____

Doodle Space

Do you like camping or staying in a hotel more? Why?

_____

_____

_____

_____

_____

_____

_____

_____

Doodle Space

Do you like camping or staying in a hotel more? Why?

_____

_____

_____

_____

_____

_____

_____

_____

_____

Doodle Space

What is something you would like to learn if you had a chance?

_____

_____

_____

_____

_____

_____

_____

_____

_____

Doodle Space

What is something you would like to learn if you had a chance?

_____

_____

_____

_____

_____

_____

_____

_____

Doodle Space

What do you think is my favorite color? Why?

_____

_____

_____

_____

_____

_____

_____

_____

_____

Doodle Space

What do you think is my favorite color? Why?

_____

_____

_____

_____

_____

_____

_____

_____

_____

Doodle Space

Do you like to sleep on your back, side or stomach? Do you like lots of pillows or not when you sleep?

_____

_____

_____

_____

_____

_____

_____

_____

_____

Doodle Space

Do you like to sleep on your back, side or stomach? Do you like lots of pillows or not when you sleep?

_____

_____

_____

_____

_____

_____

_____

_____

Doodle Space

Do you like to take showers or baths? Why?

_____

_____

_____

_____

_____

_____

_____

_____

_____

Doodle Space

Do you like to take showers or baths? Why?

_____

_____

_____

_____

_____

_____

_____

_____

_____

Doodle Space

Do you think you eat a healthy diet? Why or why not?

_____

_____

_____

_____

_____

_____

_____

_____

_____

Doodle Space

Do you think you eat a healthy diet? Why or why not?

_____

_____

_____

_____

_____

_____

_____

_____

_____

Doodle Space

What is your favorite thing about our home?

_____

_____

_____

_____

_____

_____

_____

_____

_____

Doodle Space

What is your favorite thing about our home?

_____

_____

_____

_____

_____

_____

_____

_____

_____

Doodle Space

If you could ask your grandma or grandpa to teach you anything, what would it be and why?

_____

_____

_____

_____

_____

_____

_____

_____

_____

Doodle Space

If you could ask your grandma or grandpa to teach you anything, what would it be and why?

_____

_____

_____

_____

_____

_____

_____

_____

_____

Doodle Space

Do you like living in this time in history? Why or why not? If not, when would you rather live?

_____

_____

_____

_____

_____

_____

_____

_____

_____

Doodle Space

Do you like living in this time in history? Why or why not? If not, when would you rather live?

_____

_____

_____

_____

_____

_____

_____

_____

_____

Doodle Space

What is the silliest thing you've ever done? Did anyone see you do it?

_____

_____

_____

_____

_____

_____

_____

_____

_____

Doodle Space

What is the silliest thing you've ever done? Did anyone see you do it?

_____

_____

_____

_____

_____

_____

_____

_____

_____

_____

Doodle Space

Would you rather do in a race: swim, bike or run? Is that the skill you're best at?

_____

_____

_____

_____

_____

_____

_____

_____

_____

Doodle Space

Would you rather do in a race: swim, bike or run? Is that the skill you're best at?

_____

_____

_____

_____

_____

_____

_____

_____

_____

Doodle Space

What is your favorite fairy tale and why?

_____

_____

_____

_____

_____

_____

_____

_____

_____

_____

Doodle Space

What is your favorite fairy tale and why?

_____

_____

_____

_____

_____

_____

_____

_____

_____

Doodle Space

Do you think you would like living without electricity? What would be the easiest part and what would be the hardest?

_____

_____

_____

_____

_____

_____

_____

_____

_____

Doodle Space

Do you think you would like living without electricity? What would be the easiest part and what would be the hardest?

_____

_____

_____

_____

_____

_____

_____

_____

_____

Doodle Space

What is your favorite thing about your bedroom? Why?

_____

_____

_____

_____

_____

_____

_____

_____

_____

Doodle Space

What is your favorite thing about your bedroom? Why?

_____

_____

_____

_____

_____

_____

_____

_____

_____

Doodle Space

If you could have any kind of collection, what would you collect?

_____

_____

_____

_____

_____

_____

_____

_____

_____

Doodle Space

If you could have any kind of collection, what would you collect?

_____

_____

_____

_____

_____

_____

_____

_____

_____

Doodle Space

Do you think it is more important to have lots of friends or a few really good friends? Who are your best friends?

_____

_____

_____

_____

_____

_____

_____

_____

_____

Doodle Space

Do you think it is more important to have lots of friends or a few really good friends? Who are your best friends?

_____

_____

_____

_____

_____

_____

_____

_____

_____

Doodle Space

Do you prefer taking a road trip or going on an airplane? What do you like least about the one you chose?

_____

_____

_____

_____

_____

_____

_____

_____

_____

Doodle Space

Do you prefer taking a road trip or going on an airplane? What do you like least about the one you chose?

_____

_____

_____

_____

_____

_____

_____

_____

_____

Doodle Space

Is there a smell that makes you feel warm and cozy inside? What is it?

_____

_____

_____

_____

_____

_____

_____

_____

_____

Doodle Space

Is there a smell that makes you feel warm and cozy inside? What is it?

_____

_____

_____

_____

_____

_____

_____

_____

_____

Doodle Space

What do you think is my favorite dessert? Why do you think I like it so much?

_____

_____

_____

_____

_____

_____

_____

_____

_____

Doodle Space

What do you think is my favorite dessert? Why do you think I like it so much?

_____

_____

_____

_____

_____

_____

_____

_____

Doodle Space

Do you think you would like to live in the same place forever or move around every few years? Why?

_____

_____

_____

_____

_____

_____

_____

_____

_____

Doodle Space

Do you think you would like to live in the same place forever or move around every few years? Why?

_____

_____

_____

_____

_____

_____

_____

_____

_____

Doodle Space

If you could only have 3 three things to take on a long trip (besides your clothes and essentials like toothbrush and comb/hairbrush), what would you bring and why?

_____

_____

_____

_____

_____

_____

_____

_____

Doodle Space

If you could only have 3 three things to take on a long trip (besides your clothes and essentials like toothbrush and comb/hairbrush), what would you bring and why?

_____

_____

_____

_____

_____

_____

_____

_____

_____

Doodle Space

Have you ever been asked to do something that you knew what wrong? What was it and what did you do?

_____

_____

_____

_____

_____

_____

_____

_____

Doodle Space

Have you ever been asked to do something that you knew what wrong? What was it and what did you do?

_____

_____

_____

_____

_____

_____

_____

_____

_____

Doodle Space

What has been your favorite thing you learned about me in this book? Would you like to do another book like this?

_____

_____

_____

_____

_____

_____

_____

_____

_____

Doodle Space

What has been your favorite thing you learned about me in this book? Would you like to do another book like this?

_____

_____

_____

_____

_____

_____

_____

_____

_____

Doodle Space

ABOUT THE AUTHOR

M. Susan T. Whitehead is a traveling gypsy at heart who is most "at home" experiencing new countries and cultures with her husband of 20 years, Michael, and their 6 children. She loves finding new traditions to incorporate into her family's schedule in an effort to bring a little bit of familiarity to her day, no matter what time zone she's in. Aside from traveling, Susan enjoys learning new things, watching comedy videos on YouTube and dark chocolate with almonds.

Printed in Great Britain
by Amazon